BRO...
WI...

A book of double-puzzles
to amuse you – and your friends.
Try them and see how WIDE AWAKE
you really are!

**1st MIDWAY
BROWNIE GUIDE
PACK**

Also by Rosalie Brown

BROWNIES MAKE THINGS No. 1
BROWNIES MAKE THINGS No. 2
BROWNIES MAKE THINGS No. 3
BROWNIES MAKE THINGS No. 4
HANDCRAFTS FOR ALL SEASONS No. 2
HANDCRAFTS FOR ALL SEASONS No. 3
HANDCRAFTS FOR ALL SEASONS No. 4
IDEAS FOR PACKS
MORE IDEAS FOR PACKS
THINGS TO MAKE FROM THIN CARD No. 1
THINGS TO MAKE FROM THIN CARD No. 2
BROWNIES ARE WIDE AWAKE No. 1
THINGS TO MAKE
MORE THINGS TO MAKE
HOW TO MAKE MASKS AND PARTY HATS
MORE MASKS AND PARTY HATS
HOW TO MAKE YOUR OWN DECORATIONS
HOW TO MAKE YOUR OWN GREETING CARDS
HOW TO MAKE PAPER CUTS AND SILHOUETTES
GAMES FOR TRAVELLERS

With Arthur Brown

HOW TO MAKE AND PLAY INDOOR GAMES No. 1
HOW TO MAKE AND PLAY INDOOR GAMES No. 2
HOW TO MAKE AND PLAY INDOOR GAMES No. 3

BROWNIES ARE WIDE AWAKE

No. 2

Jade Publishers
15 Stoatley Rise
Haslemere
Surrey   GU27 1AF

First published 1977
Reprinted 1978

First published in this revised edition 1989

© Copyright Rosalie Brown 1977, 1989
Cover design © Copyright Jade Publishers 1989

All rights reserved. No part of this publication may be reproduced, stored in a retrieval system, or transmitted in any form or by any means, electronic, mechanical, photocopying, recording or otherwise without the prior written permission of the publishers. This book is sold subject to the condition that it shall not, by way of trade or otherwise be lent, re-sold, hired out or otherwise circulated without the publisher's prior consent in any form of binding or cover other than that in which it is published and without a similar condition including this condition being imposed on the subsequent purchaser.

Cover illustration by Brendan Catney
Cover lettering by Jim Wire

Typeset by 'Keyword', New Cottage, Trooper Road, Aldbury, Tring, Herts, HP23 5RW

Printed and bound by Bocardo Press Ltd, Didcot.

British Library Cataloguing in Publication Data
Brown, Rosalie, *1910—*
Brownies are wide awake.
2.
1. Puzzles. Collections for children
I.Title
793.73

ISBN 0–903461–12–9

BROWNIES ARE WIDE AWAKE

No. 2

Devised and drawn

by

ROSALIE BROWN

Published in conjunction with
The Girl Guides Association

JADE PUBLISHERS
HASLEMERE

HOW·MANY·OF·THESE·WILD FLOWERS·DO·YOU·KNOW

1.	5.
2.	6.
3.	7.
4.	8.

LOOK AT PUZZLE ONE TO HELP YOU HERE

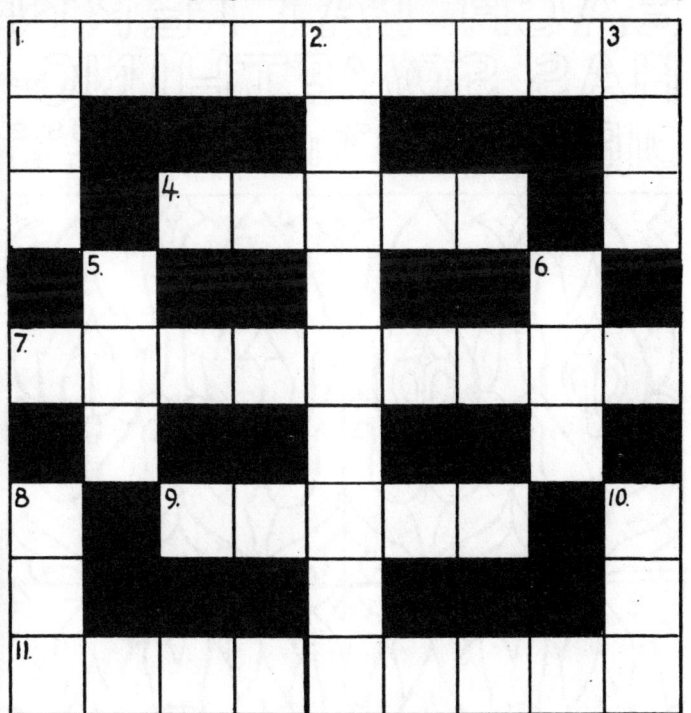

ACROSS.
1. Blue woodland flower.
4. Coloured part of flowers.
7. Number '4' flower'.
9. Some plants grow on r····
11. Some larger garden Flowers are like 'Number 8.'

DOWN.
1. This comes before flowers.
2. Flower 'Number .1'.
3. Petals open when ··· shines.
5. Put flowers in a ··· of water.
6. Seeds can be in a ···
8. 1st. half of 'No.5's'. name.
10. Month with a flower name.

EACH PATTERN HAS SOMETHING DIFFERENT IN IT.

CAN YOU SEE WHAT IT IS?

1.	3.
2.	4.

PATTERNS can be used on many things.

Can you work out the list here?

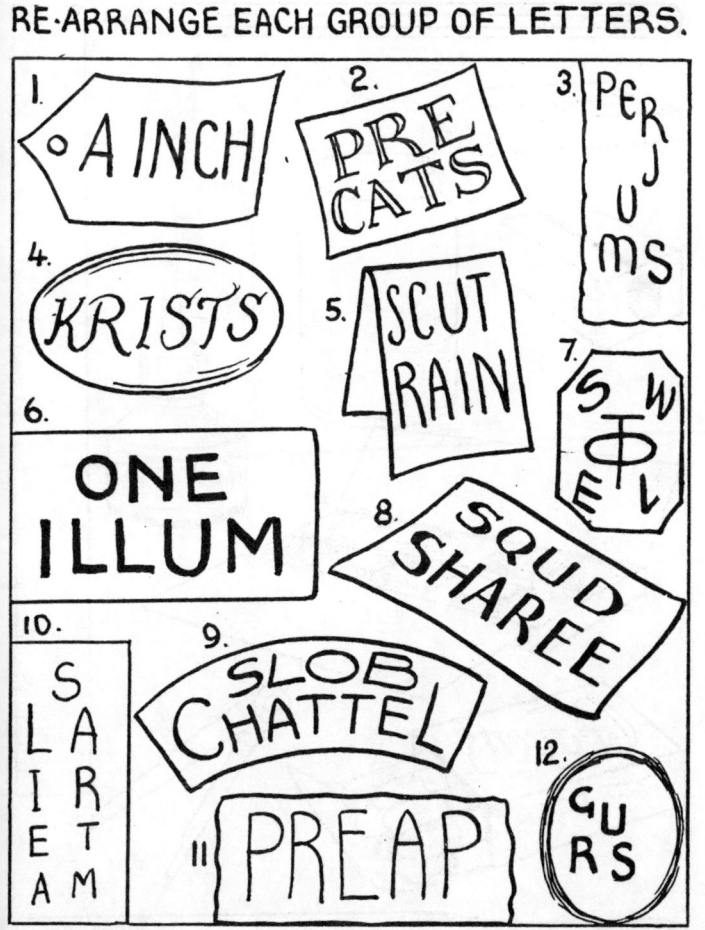

RE-ARRANGE EACH GROUP OF LETTERS.

1. A INCH
2. PRE CATS
3. PER JUMS
4. KRISTS
5. SCUT RAIN
6. ONE ILLUM
7. S W E V
8. SQUD SHAREE
9. SLOB CHATTEL
10. S L I E A S A R T M
11. PREAP
12. GURS

LOOK AT THESE FOR 3 MINUTES THEN COVER THE PAGE. WRITE DOWN ALL YOU CAN REMEMBER.

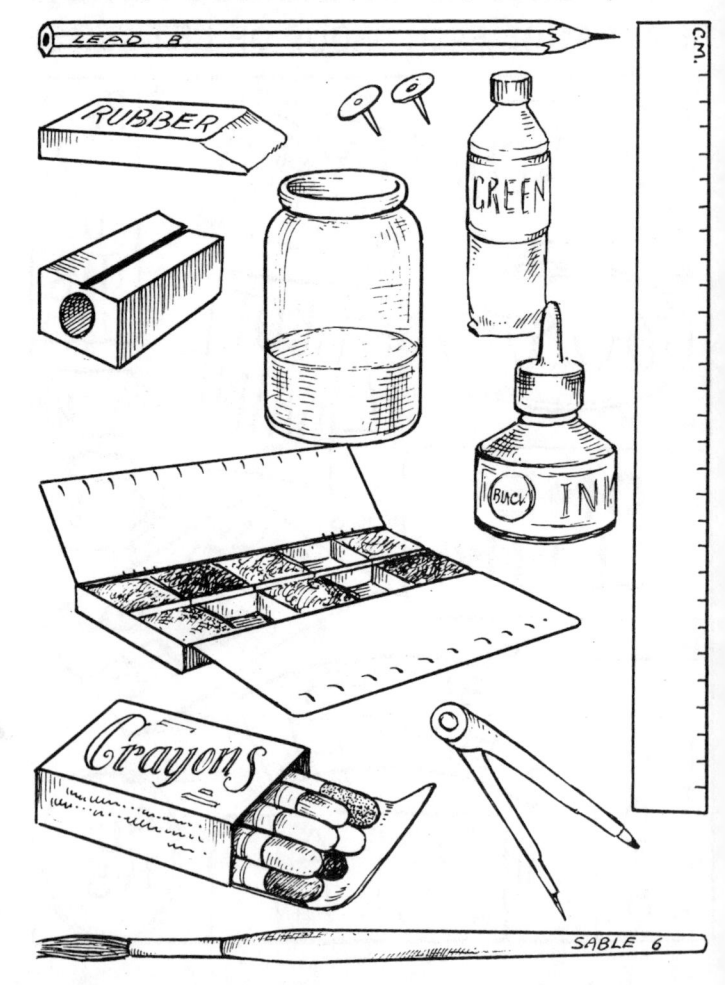

CHECK YOUR LIST OF THINGS IN PUZZLE 5. WITH THE DRAWINGS

How many things were there.
Did you get them all?

Now cover that page up again
and answer these questions.

←Hold a mirror on this line→

6. WHAT WORDS ON THE PENCIL.

THE RULER.

5. WHAT MARKINGS WERE ON

4. HOW MANY CRAYONS IN BOX.

3. WAS THE WATER JAR FULL.

2. HOW MANY PAINTS IN BOX.

1. WAS THE BRUSH IN A POINT.

SEASONS

Each figure spells a season, can you work them out.

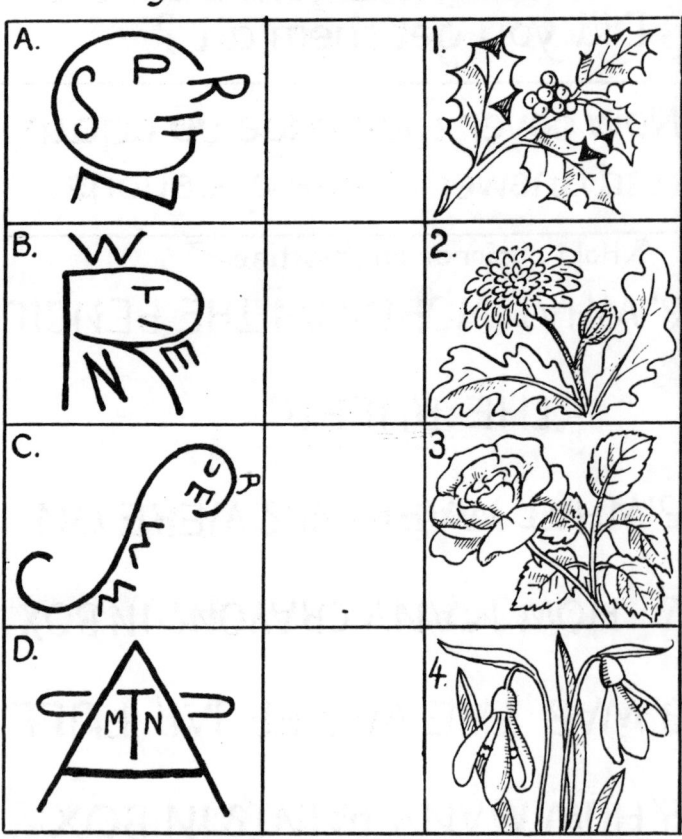

A. SPRING		1. (holly)
B. WINTER		2. (chrysanthemum)
C. SUMMER		3. (rose)
D. AUTUMN		4. (snowdrops)

Draw a line from each season to the flower which is in bloom at that time.

FESTIVALS

In each circle, starting at the white letters miss every second letter and spell out four festivals

Write the name of the seasons here ↓	Write the season's festival here. ↓
A.	
B.	
C.	
D.	

WHAT IS HAPPENING HERE

DRAW LINES FROM DOT 1. TO DOT 71. TO FIND OUT.

DRAW IN THE
FACE AND ANY
OTHER MISSING
PARTS

HERE ARE OTHER KINDS OF DANCES

WRITE IN THE MISSING VOWELS

1. P.LK. (POLKA)
2. T.NG. (TANGO)
3. M.RR.S (MORRIS)
4. H.RNP.P. (HORNPIPE)
5. B.LL.R..M. (BALLROOM)
6. R..L (REEL)
7. J.G (JIG)
8. M.N..T (MINUET)
9. M.YP.L. (MAYPOLE)
10. F.XTR.T (FOXTROT)

1.	2.	3.
4.	5.	
6.	7.	8.
9.	10.	

IN WHICH COUNTRIES MIGHT YOU SEE THESE THINGS

1.
2.
3.
4.

IF YOU DO NOT KNOW ALL THE COUNTRIES IN PUZZLE .II.

This page will help you if you finish off the letters in each word.

Large jumping animal →	KANGAROO
It is found in →	AUSTRALIA
This lady had a fish tail →	THE LITTLE MERMAID
She can be seen by the sea in →	DENMARK
This building is worked by wind →	WINDMILL
They can be seen in →	HOLLAND
Tall poles. Red Indian carve them →	TOTEMS
Seen in many places in →	CANADA

WHAT IS WRONG
with all of these drawings?

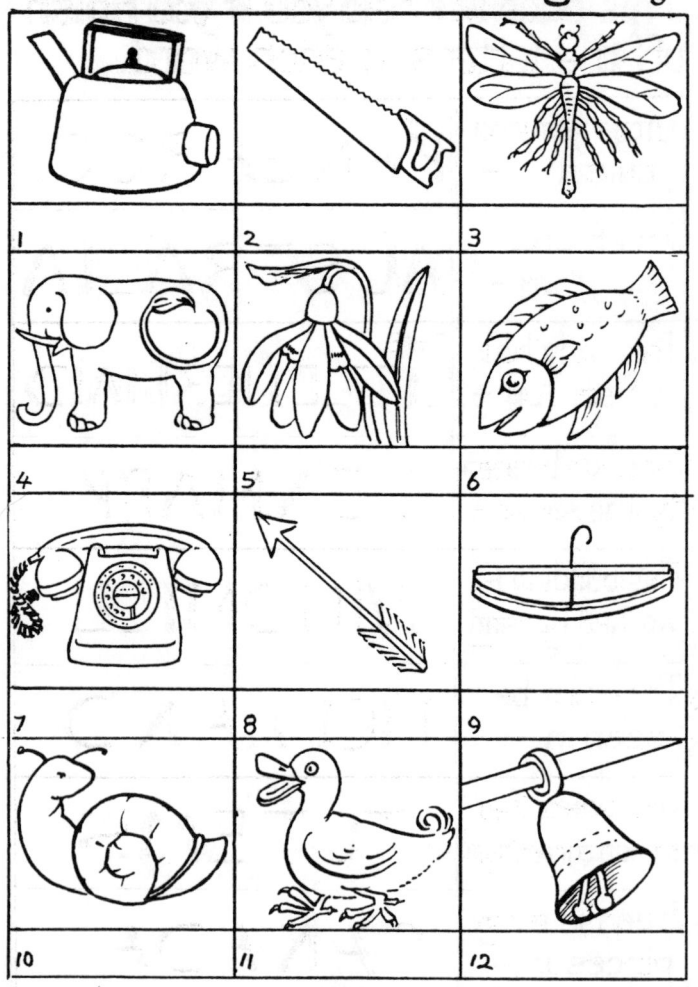

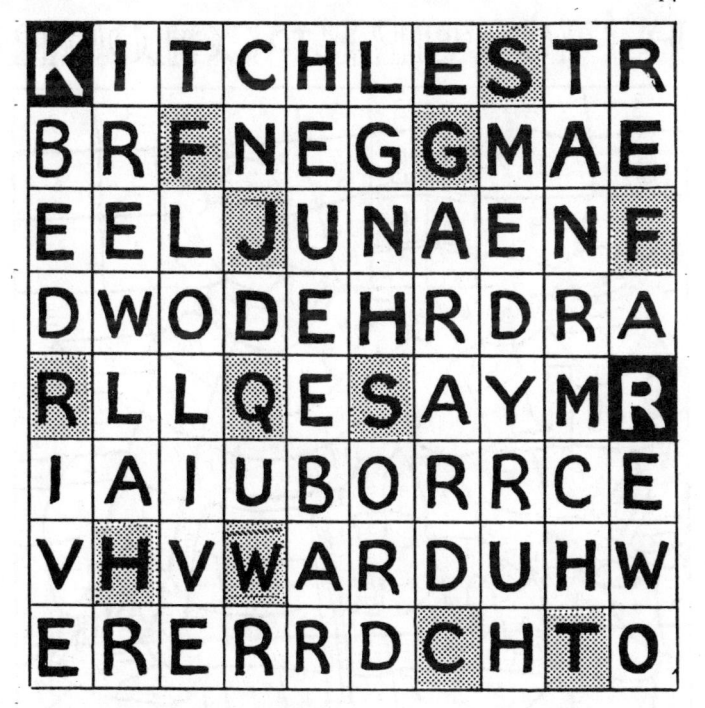

K	I	T	C	H	L	E	S	T	R
B	R	F	N	E	G	G	M	A	E
E	E	L	J	U	N	A	E	N	F
D	W	O	D	E	H	R	D	R	A
R	L	L	Q	E	S	A	Y	M	R
I	A	I	U	B	O	R	R	C	E
V	H	V	W	A	R	D	U	H	W
E	R	E	R	R	D	C	H	T	O

WHERE WILL YOU FIND

ALL THE THINGS IN PUZZLE 13 ? Start at **K** move to the right, left, or up and down but NEVER at an angle to see where to find them. Finish at **R** To help you each word begins with a shaded letter.

A PICTURE TO COLOUR

1 – BROWN. 2 – GREY. 3 – SKY BLUE. 4 – DARK GREEN.
5 – GRASS GREEN. 6 – RED. 7 – LIGHT BROWN. 8 – FLESH.

"PUZZLE 15 WILL HELP YOU

Write all your answers in this grid. Some of the first letters are written in to help you.

WHAT DOES THE SHADED LINE READ.

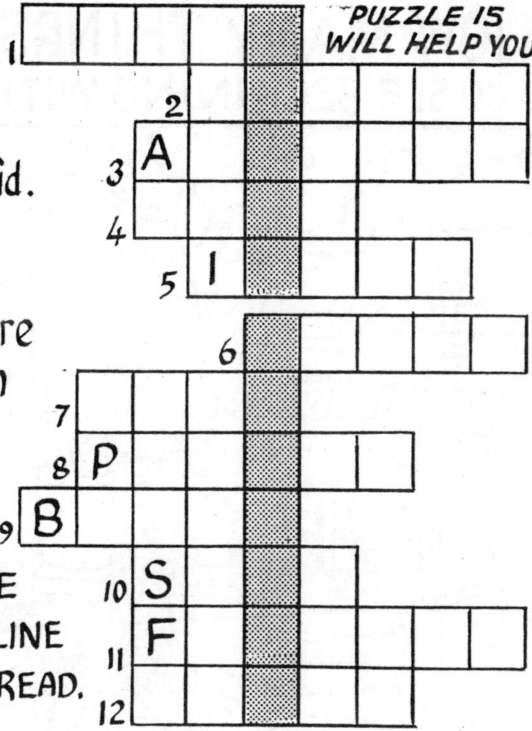

NOW FINISH OFF THESE LETTERS →

1. He did not wear .....
2. Animal in picture.
3. He loved all ....
4. The dove is on his ....
5. His home was in .....
6. Another name for monk.
7. He helped .... people.
8. Travelled far to ...... to the people.
9. Colour of his habit.
10. He also tended the..
11. All creatures were his..
12. The Man he spoke about.

HOW MANY THINGS CAN
YOU SEE BEGINNING WITH A .T.

Fill in this crossword using words beginning with **T** found in puzzle 17.

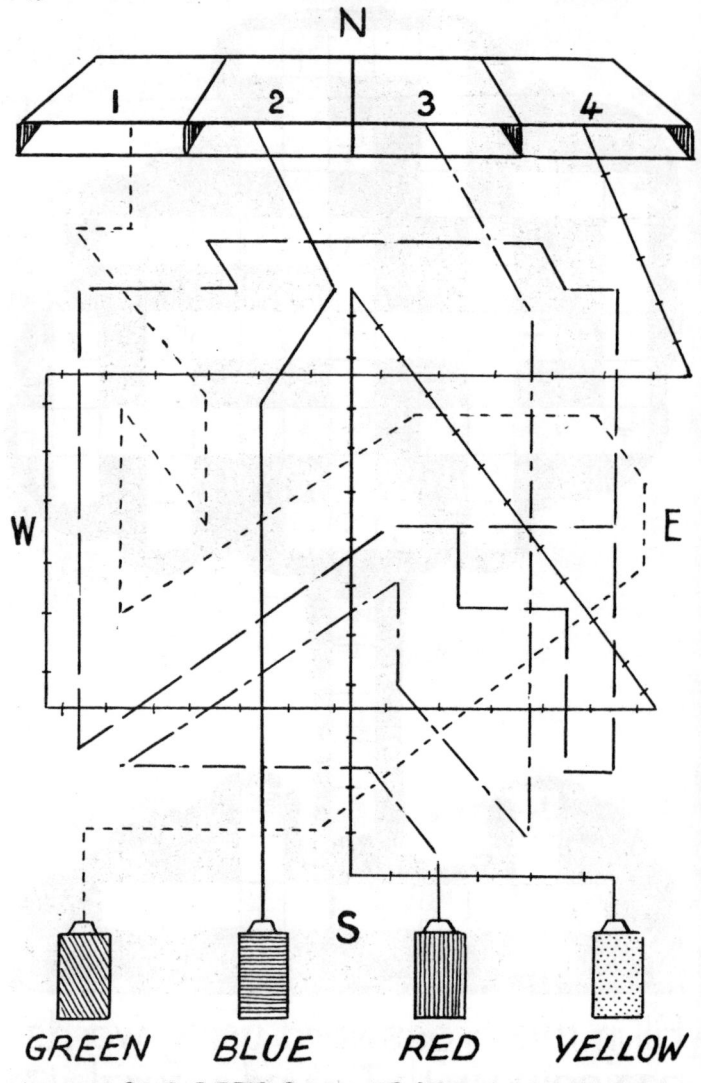

WHICH BUS GETS BACK TO ITS GARAGE FIRST.

LOOK AT PUZZLE 19

N
W
E
S

ACROSS
3. Which bus had the shortest run.
4. Which bus turned back towards S. on its run.
5. How many turns did the green bus make.
8. Number of green bus.
9. Number of blue bus.
10. What compass point is on right.
11. What point is at the top.
12. Have all lines a bus.
13. Point on the left.

DOWN
1. Bus with longest run.
2. Which was on dotted line.
6. Bottom compass point.
7. Number of yellow bus.
9. Red bus number.

COLOURS

DO YOU KNOW THE COLOURS IN YOUR PAINT BOX, AND HOW TO MIX THEM TO MAKE NEW COLOURS

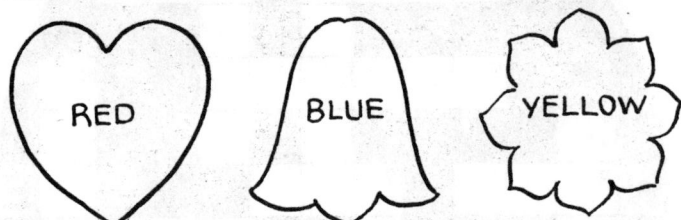

RED BLUE YELLOW

These three colours are the important ones. They are called PRIMARY COLOURS. Mix any two together to make a new colour. Colour all these shapes in.

blue and yellow makes green

yellow and red makes orange

red and blue makes purple

Mix all three together to make a brown

HAVE YOU COLOURED THE SHAPES.

WILL PUZZLE 21 HELP YOU?

Across
1. Red and blue makes .....
3. Artists .... their work.
7. One kind of paint.
9. Keep your ..... clean.
10. Red and yellow makes ..
11. Last colour mentioned.
14. Use this to paint on.
15. Dirty water, ... colours.
16. A primary colour.

Down
1. Chalk colours.
2. To wipe brushes clean.
4. Never put this away dirty.
5. Always use ....
6. Blue and yellow makes ..
8. Paint box not in use.
12. Another kind of paint.
13. A primary colour.

DO YOU KNOW THESE ROAD SIGNS. Colour them correctly

1.
2.
3.
4 and 5
6.
7.
8.
9.
10.
11 and 12
13.

you all know this one →

RED. GREEN. WHITE. BLACK. BLUE. AMBER

STOP CHILDREN

24

1.		1		25			2		19	
2.							10			
3.			3					5		
4, 5.					15	9				16
6.			20	22						
7 {			17	6			11			
							14			
8.					13					
9.				18	12	23		4		
10					24			21		
11, 12		8					7			

1	2	3	4	5

6	7	8

9	10	11	12	13	14	15	16

17	18	19

20	21	22	23	24	25

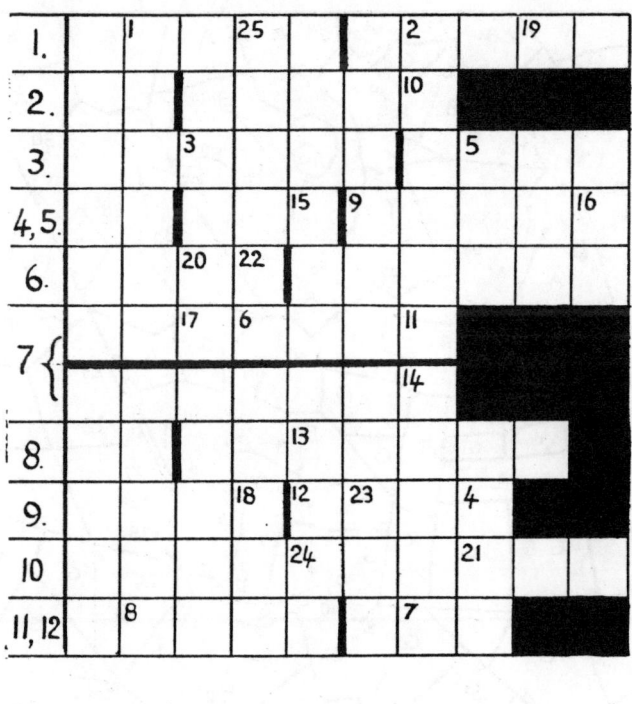

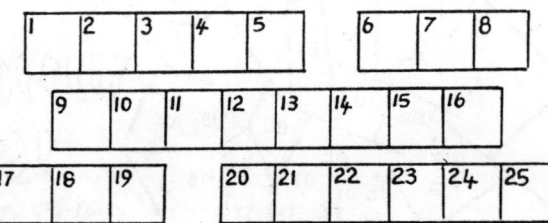

Write the signs of Puzzle 23 in the numbered lines. Now write all the letters with numbers in the box with the same number. This will tell you what sign 13 is.

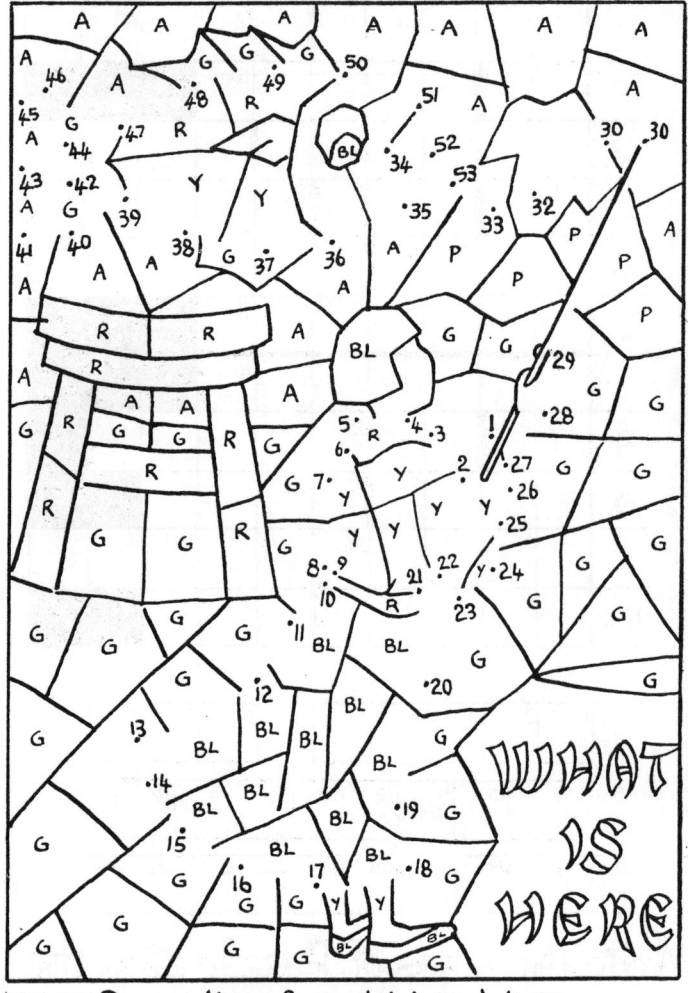

FIRST. Drawn lines from dot 1 to dot 53.
SECOND. Colour the picture. BL—BLACK. R—RED.
A—PALE BLUE. P—PURPLE. G—GREEN. Y—YELLOW.

26

The name of this country	10	1 A	16	1	14			
The child is flying a	6	9	19	8	11	9	20	5
The mountain is called	6	21	10	9	25	1	13	1
The girls wear a	11	9	13	15	14	15		
They are fond of this plant and often draw it.	3 C	8	5	18	18	25		
	2 B	12	15	19	19	15	13	
There are many of these	20	5	13	16	12	5	19	
Some statues are	2	21	4	4	8	1		
Japan is in this sea	16	1	3	9	6	9	3	
This is the Capital	20	15	11	25	15			

WRITE THE ALPHABET IN THESE BOXES.

1. A	2. B	3. C	4.	5.	6.	7.	8.	9.	10.
11.	12.	13.	14.	15.	16.	17.	18.	19.	20.
		21.	22.	23.	24.	25.	26.		

TO FIND THE ANSWERS TO THE QUESTIONS WRITE THE LETTERS WITH NUMBERS IN THE SAME NUMBERED BOXES ABOVE.

CURIOUS BILLS
HAVE YOU SEEN ANY OF THEM ??

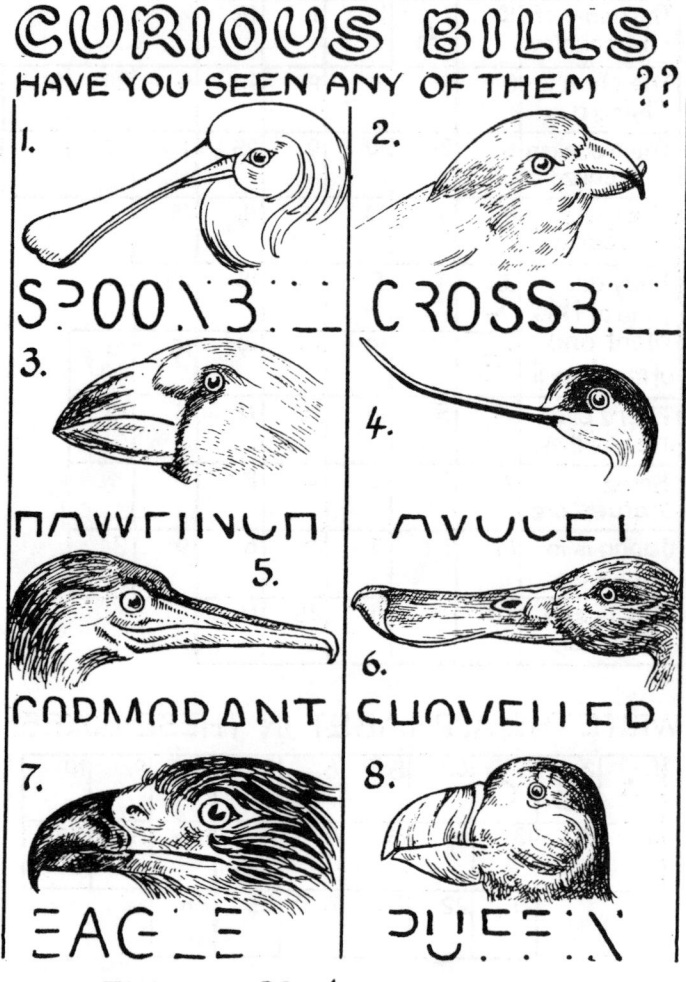

1. SPOONB___

2. CROSSB___

3. HAWFINCH

4. AVOCET

5. CORMORANT

6. SHOVELLER

7. EAGLE

8. PUFFIN

Finish off the names.
1 and 2 missing down strokes. 3,4 top halves.
5,6 bottom halves. 7,8 down strokes.

Muddled Letters

Re-arrange the words to tell you
A. Where each bird is found.
B. One thing each bird feeds on.

1. VERRI THOUM a. R M SPOLDATE b. T	2. IRF SWODO a. NOCE DEESS b.
3. DOWDNOAL a. W YERRCH NOTESS b. C S	4. TRAWE a. SPIRMSH b. S
5. EAS a. TALF SHIF b. F	6. SKALE a. TRAWE PLSNTA b.
7. SDNALHGIH a. H SERAH b.	8. AES FFLICS a. SLLAM SHIF b.

THE FIRST LETTER OF SOME WORDS HAVE BEEN WRITTEN IN TO HELP YOU.

FINISH OFF THESE TOOLS OF TRADE.
Write what they are at the bottom.

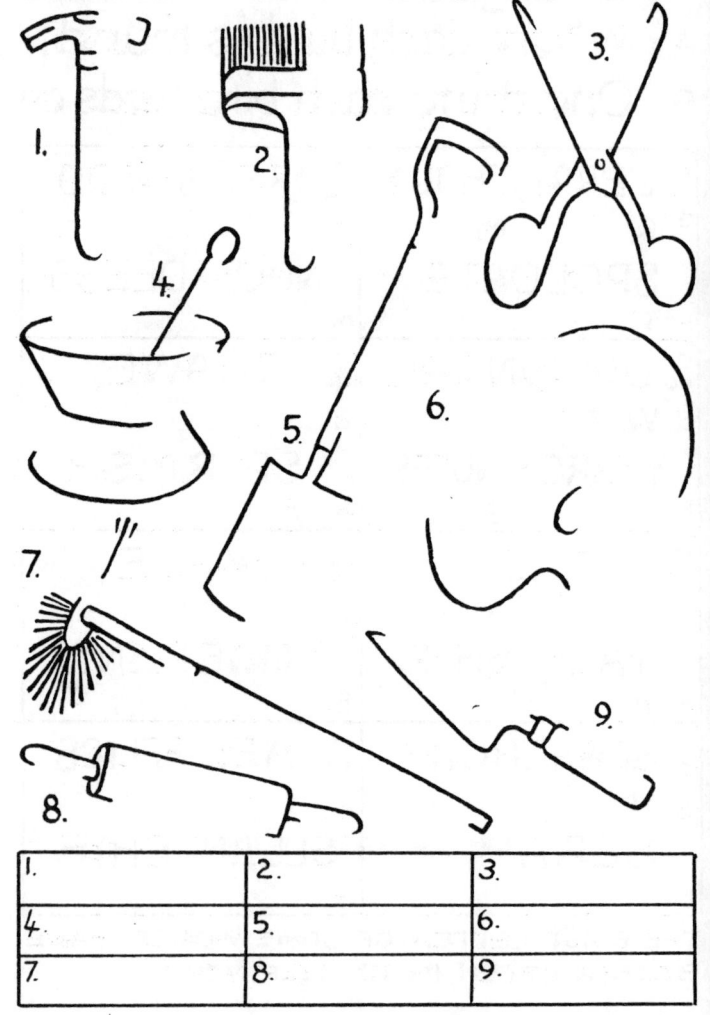

1.	2.	3.
4.	5.	6.
7.	8.	9.

TRADES OF ALL KINDS ~

Work out these names of trade then underneath each one write the tool in puzzle 29 each person would use.

1. HESUO PRATNEI
2. PSWEE
3. OKC
4. RENIOJ
5. CH·M·ST
6. GARDENER
7. ARTICT
8. TAILOR
9. BUILDER

Now draw a line from these objects to each of the names above.

HERE ARE FOUR NAMES OF OVERSEAS COUNTRIES

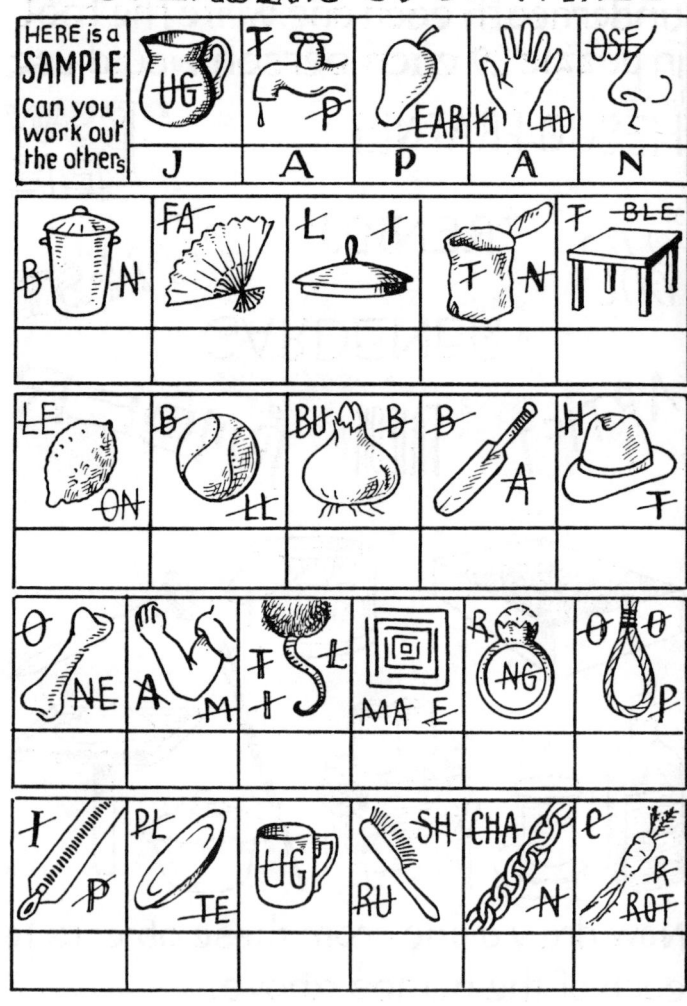

HERE is a SAMPLE — Can you work out the others?

Sample: **J A P A N**

I	N	D	I	A
M	A	L	T	A
B	R	A	Z	I	L
Z	A	M	B	I	A

ISLANDS ROUND THE WORLD

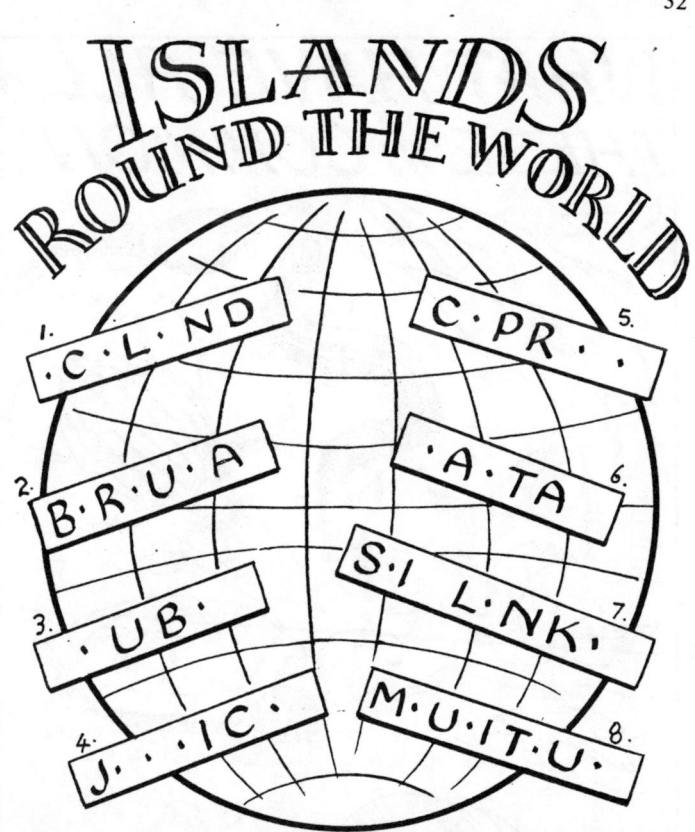

1. ·C·L·ND·
2. B·R·U·A
3. ·UB·
4. J···IC·
5. C·PR··
6. ·A·TA
7. S·I·L·NK·
8. M·U·IT·U·

AAAAAAAA C D EE II L MMM RR SS U Y   THESE ARE THE MISSING LETTERS.   CAN YOU FIT THEM IN?

1.	5.
2.	6.
3.	7.
4.	8.

WHAT HAVE ALL THESE IN COMMON?

LOOK AT PUZZLE 34 FOR THE ANSWER

THEY ARE ALL SAMES

HOLD THIS PAGE LEVEL WITH YOUR EYES

HAVE YOU A PET LIKE THIS?

Draw a line from dot to dot, starting at 1. Finish at 49.

Can you finish it off and colour it in?

Unscramble these letters and spell out what the pet is.

DEGGIURRBA

Pets

Write down all the letters in these figures and sort each one out to spell a pet.

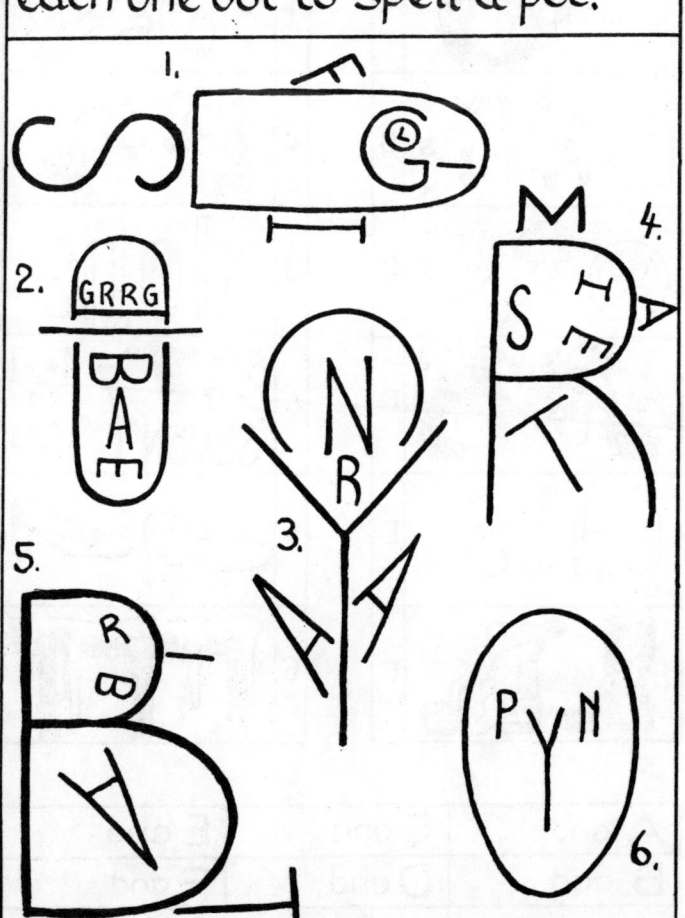

1. S, F, G, L, I, H
2. G, R, R, G, B, A, E
3. N, R, A, A
4. M, S, H, E, A, T
5. R, B, A, L, B, D
6. P, Y, N, Y

CAN YOU PAIR THESE TOGETHER

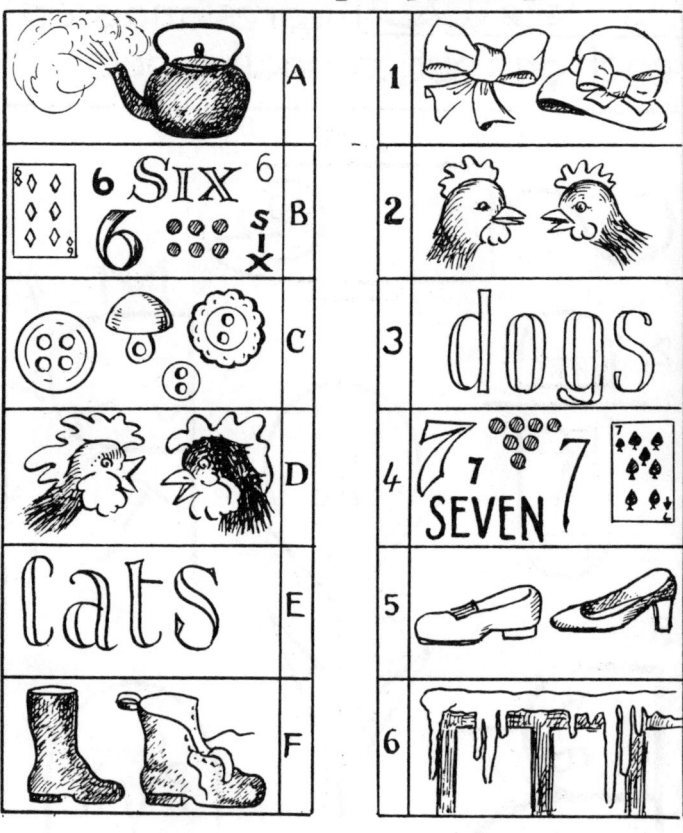

A and	C and	E and
B and	D and	F and

38

USE THE PAIRS AND ANYTHING ELSE YOU SEE IN PUZZLE 37 TO HELP YOU FILL THIS PUZZLE

Some letters are written in to start you off

ANSWERS

Puzzle No:

1. (1) Buttercup. (2) Clover. (3) Daisy. (4) Dandelion.
   (5) Cowslip. (6) Primrose. (7) Periwinkle. (8) Poppy.

2. *Across:* (1) Bluebell. (4) Petal. (7) Dandelion. (9) Rocks.
   (11) Wild poppy.
   Down: (1) Bud. (2) Buttercup. (3) Sun. (5) Jar. (6) Pod.
   (8) Cow. (10) May.

3. (1) Centres. (2) Leaves at bottom. (3) Extra points round centre.
   (4) Bottoms of centre part.

4. (1) China. (2) Carpets. (3) Jumpers. (4) Skirts.
   (5) Curtains. (6) Linoleum. (7) Towels. (8) Head-squares.
   (9) Tablecloths. (10) Materials. (11) Paper. (12) Rugs.

5. Look at these articles.

6. Twelve things.
   (1) No. (2) Ten. (3) No. (4) Seven. (5) C.M. (6) Lead B.

7. A. Spring   – 4 (Snowdrops)
   B. Winter   – 1 (Holly)
   C. Summer – 3 (Rose)
   D. Autumn – 2 (Chrysanthemum)

8. A. Spring. – Easter.
   B. Summer. – Midsummers Day.
   C. Autumn. – Hallowe'en.
   D. Winter. – Christmas Day.

9. A Dancer.

10. (1) Polka. (2) Tango. (3) Morris. (4) Hornpipe. (5) Ballroom.
    (6) Square. (7) Waltz. (8) Minuet. (9) Maypole. (10) Fox Trot.

11. (1) Australia. (2) Denmark. (3) Holland. (4) Canada.

12. Kangaroo – Australia. The Little Mermaid – Denmark.
    Windmill – Holland. Totems – Canada.

13. (1) Kettle spout too high up. (2) Saw edge wrong side.
    (3) Too many legs. (4) Wrong kind of tail. (5) Too many
    petals (should be only three). (6) Fins should point backwards. (7) Wire on earpiece. (8) Feathers pointing wrong
    way. (9) Hook wrong way up. (10) Shell wrong way round.

(11) Feet should be webbed. (12) Should only be one 'tongue'.
14. (1) Kitchen. (2) Flower bed. (3) River. (4) Hall. (5) Quiver. (6) Wardrobe. (7) Shed. (8) Jungle. (9) Stream. (10) Garden. (11) Farmyard. (12) Church tower.
15. 'A picture to colour.'
16. (1) Shoes. (2) Rabbit. (3) Animals. (4) Hand. (5) Italy. (6) Friar. (7) Poor. (8) Preach. (9) Brown. (10) Sick. (11) Friends. (12) Jesus.
Shaded and half letters read: SAINT FRANCIS OF ASSISI.
17. Tree. Trunk. Thatch. Tap. Tadpoles. Tents. Tower. Table. Tablecloth. Tie. Trousers. Teeth. Tail. Toes. Tray. Traycloth. Tea cup. Teapot. Tea. Teaspoons. Tortoise. Tennis bats. Tennis balls. Trellis. Thorns. Thigh. Thistle. (27).
18. *Across:* (1) Tents. (3) Tie. (4) Tap. (6) Thatch. (7) Tennis bat. (10) Table. (11) Tadpoles. (12) Tea. (16) Tennis balls.
Down: (1) Tail. (2) Thigh. (4) Teapot. (5) Trellis. (6) Thistle. (8) Thorn. (9) Toes. (13) Table. (14) Tree. (15) Tray.
19. The Blue bus.
20. *Across:* (3) Blue. (4) Red. (5) Twelve. (8) One. (9) Two. (10) East. (11) North. (12) No. (13) West.
Down: (1) Yellow. (2) Green. (6) South. (7) Four. (9) Three.
21. 'Colours.'
22. *Across:* (1) Purple. (3) Sign. (7) Watercolour. (9) Hands. (10) Orange. (11) Brown. (14) Paper.. (15) Dull. (16) Blue.
Down: (1) Pastels. (2) Rag. (4) Paintbrush. (5) Clean water. (6) Green. (8) Shut. (12) Oil. (13) Red.
23. Colour these road signs.
24. (1) Cross Roads. (2) No Entry. (3) Double Bend. (4) & (5) Do Not Cross. (6) Hump Bridge. (7) Traffic Signals. (8) No Waiting. (9) Turn Left. (10) Roundabout. (11) & (12) Cross Now. Sign 13: ROUTE FOR CYCLISTS AND MOPEDS.
25. Child with a fish kite.
26. *From the top:* Japan. Fish kite. Fujiyama. Kimono. Cherry. Blossom. Temples. Buddha. Pacific. Tokyo.

27. (1) Spoonbill. (2) Crossbill. (3) Hawfinch. (4) Avocet. (5) Cormorant. (6) Shoveller. (7) Eagle. (8) Puffin.

28. (1a) River. Mouth. (b) Tadpoles.
    (2a) Fir Woods. (b) Cone Seeds.
    (3a) Woodlands. (b) Cherry stones.
    (4a) Water. (b) Shrimps.
    (5a) Sea. (b) Flatfish.
    (6a) Lakes. (b) Water plants.
    (7a) Highlands. (b) Hares.
    (8a) Sea cliffs. (b) Small fish.

29. (1) Hammer. (2) Painter's brush. (3) Scissors. (4) Pestle and mortar. (5) Spade. (6) Palette. (7) Chimney brush. (8) Rolling pin. (9) Plaster trowel.

30. (1) House painter uses 2. Tin of paint.
    (2) Sweep uses 7.   Chimneys.
    (3) Cook uses 8.   Cake.
    (4) Joiner uses 1.   Nail.
    (5) Chemist uses 4.   Medicine bottle.
    (6) Gardener uses 5.   Box of seedlings.
    (7) Artist uses 6.   Paint brush.
    (8) Tailor uses 3.   Needle and thread.
    (9) Builder uses 9.   Cement.

31. India. Malta. Brazil. Zambia.

32. (1) Iceland. (2) Bermuda. (3) Cuba. (4) Jamaica. (5) Cyprus. (6) Malta. (7) Sri Lanka. (8) Mauritius.

33/34. They are all swimmers.

35. Budgerigar.

36. (1) Goldfish. (2) Budgerigar. (3) Canary. (4) Hamster. (5) Rabbit. (6) Pony.

37. A and 6. B and 4. C and 1. D and 2. E and 3. F and 5.

38. *Across:* (1) Cocks. (4) Cats. (6) Boots. (7) Sevens. (9) Hens. (10) Icicles. (12) Dogs.
    Down: (2) Kettle. (3) Cards. (5) Six. (6) Bows. (8) Shoes. (11) Cold.

GOOD NEWS!

Read *BROWNIE* Magazine fortnightly — now bigger, brighter and better than ever before.

There are more pages, most of them in full colour, and more for you to do and read. It is published fortnightly and costs just 50p.

Order your copy from your newsagent today.

Meet these characters and many more in BROWNIE

There is an elephant called Freda, Sarah knew she wasn't wrong. The girls all welcome Freda and greet her with a song.

Dear Newsagent,

please order me......copy(ies) of *BROWNIE* every fortnight (50p)

Name ....

Address ....

....

Signature of parent/guardian ....